30 SIMPLE ENERGY THINGS YOU CAN DO TO SAVE THE EARTH

Pacific Gas & Electric

The EarthWorks Group

THIS BOOK IS PRINTED ON RECYCLED PAPER

Created and Packaged by Javnarama
Designed by Javnarama

We've provided a great deal of practice and product information in our book. In most cases, we've relied on advice, recommendations, and research we consider accurate and free from bias. However, we can't and don't guarantee results. This book offers you a start. The responsibility for using it ultimately rests with you.

ACKNOWLEDGMENTS

The EarthWorks Group would like to thank everyone who helped to make this book possible, including:

PG&E People
- Tom Auzenne (Whose dedication and hard work made this book possible)
- Alison Silverstein (For thinking big and editing small)
- Lee Callaway
- Paul Brodie
- Charles Segerstrom

Writers
- John Javna
- Seth Zuckerman
- Chris Calwell

Friends & Experts
- Julie Bennett
- Nenelle Bunnin
- Brad Bunnin
- David Goldstein
- The Natural Resources Defense Council
- The Ecology Center
- Karina Lutz, *Home Energy* magazine
- Larry Weingarten
- 5th St. Computer Services, 1794 Fifth St., Berkeley, CA 94710. Our office away from the office. Thanks, Jay.

"Nobody made a greater mistake than he who did nothing because he could only do a little."

—Edmund Burke

A Note from the EarthWorks Group

Our original book, *50 Simple Things You Can Do to Save the Earth* deals with a wide range of environmental issues. This is a companion volume, specifically targeted to saving the Earth by saving energy.

If you've already got a copy of *50 Simple Things*, read on. Most of the info included here is new.

If you haven't seen a copy of *50 Simple Things* yet, pick one up at your local bookstore. Energy's a big piece of the environmental puzzle, but there's plenty more to learn.

There is nothing more important than cleaning up our world. But it will be a huge task. It will require the enthusiastic cooperation of every segment of our society—including government and business.

That is why we are so pleased to have prepared this book for Pacific Gas and Electric.

They've always brought power to homes and businesses. Now they're bringing power to people.

It's your move.

CONTENTS

INTRODUCTION

This book is about what we can do to change our impact on the environment by changing the way we use energy. Every use of energy has some effect on the land and water and air—so using energy more efficiently softens its impact on our planet.

30 Simple Energy Things You Can Do to Save the Earth is a new supplement to the best-selling book, *50 Simple Things You Can Do to Save the Earth*, published last year by the EarthWorks Group in Berkeley, California.

When I read *50 Simple Things*, I was impressed by the variety of steps one person can take to change his or her impact on the earth. Simple things like installing high efficiency lighting, planting a tree, changing the time that you run your air conditioner, or turning off the water a minute earlier—all can reduce the amount of energy you use. By following the simple energy conservation steps outlined in this book, you'll help hold down energy costs—today and in the years to come—and lighten the load on the environment.

As a company, Pacific Gas and Electric is committed to doing our part to protect the extraordinary beauty and character of northern and central California. And as individuals, all of us at PG&E want to work with you to preserve this land, and the planet it's part of, for all time.

Although we are one of the largest electricity generators in the country, our generation mix is among the cleanest. We use waterpower, clean-burning natural gas, geothermal steam, nuclear power, and purchases of energy from renewable, alternative energy sources like wind, solar, and biomass.

We are an industry leader in our commitment to energy efficiency and conservation. Since 1976, we've worked with our customers to weatherize millions of homes, install more energy-efficient appliances, use more energy-efficient production processes, and find ways to get more done using less energy. In the process, we've saved the equivalent of millions of barrels of oil and reduced customers' energy demand by the equivalent of two major power plants.

Our land managers watch over more than 200,000 acres of California lands, from urban corners to wilderness forests. Working with our biologists and other scientists, they preserve the character and cleanliness of 200 lakes, plant 300,000 trees every year, and protect the habitat of 150 rare, endangered and threatened plant, aquatic, and animal species.

And we're committed to doing more—in our research, in our planning, and in our day-to-day operations—to carry out our commitment to preserve and protect our environment. For example, we are making a major commitment to natural gas powered and electric vehicles to reduce air pollution.

Our actions make a difference in assuring the quality of our environment. But your actions count, too. So please work with us. Use the ideas and information in this book, because it's simple things that will ultimately make the biggest difference in saving our Earth.

Richard A. Clarke
Chairman and CEO,
Pacific Gas and Electric Company

SAVING ENERGY & THE ENVIRONMENT

Believe it or not, Pacific Gas and Electric—the people who sell you energy—have given you this book to help you use *less* energy. That's a smart move on their part; helping customers save energy is cheaper than the cost of building new pipelines and power plants. It's often cheaper than the cost of running *existing* power plants! Saving energy also reduces your monthly bills, and PG&E knows that customers with lower bills are satisfied customers.

There's another critically important reason to save energy—it's good for the planet. By reducing the emissions of "greenhouse gases" like carbon dioxide and methane, energy efficiency is our first line of defense against the "greenhouse effect." But saving energy does more than help solve huge environmental problems like the warming of the earth. It also improves that part of "the environment" that you enjoy every day.

Conserving energy makes your air easier to breathe, improves visibility on a smoggy day, and helps keep acid rain from ruining the pristine lakes where you fish and swim. By reducing the need for *new* power plants, saving energy also means damming fewer scenic lakes and rivers. It means that the land and water once marked for coal and nuclear power plants are available for something else, like public parks full of majestic old trees and soaring birds and sunny, silent meadows.

This book is about taking the first simple steps on the road to a better world. It means doing your part—whether your part includes the things that are easy, or the tougher measures. Most people, once they get started, discover a natural progression from one to the other. Once you try a few easy things—and see how much you save on your energy bill—you'll want to give the harder things a try to rack up even bigger savings.

We at the Natural Resources Defense Council (NRDC) have worked long and hard with PG&E to develop exciting new ways for its customers to save energy. We've also spent years working with lawmakers and manufacturers to make sure that the refrigerators, windows, light fixtures, furnaces, and other appliances for sale in stores are as efficient as possible.

But ultimately, it's *you* who can make the biggest difference. It's up to you to visit your local appliance dealer to find out how much energy you could save by replacing your old appliances. It's up to you to take advantage of your utility's new programs to promote compact fluorescent lightbulbs (amazing new lights that use 1/4 as much energy and last 10 times as long as regular bulbs). Just asking your local hardware store if it carries a full range of energy-saving lightbulbs and showerheads can make a difference. Any store that wants to please its customers will respond to repeated requests to carry specific new products.

So will it really make a difference if you follow the tips in this book? You bet. Last year, America spent $400 *billion* on energy. If all of us tried the kinds of things listed in this book at home, at school, and at work, we could cut that energy bill by billions!

Many of us have long thought that "environmental action" was some distant, unapproachable thing, like turning your back on civilization to commune with nature. When the problems seemed so big and the solutions so difficult, we felt like giving up. But we were wrong.

Today, "environmental action" is the sum of the little things we do every day: where we throw our bottles and cans, how we drive our cars, what we do to reduce energy use in our showers and air conditioners and stoves. You hold in your hands the first step to becoming an "energy activist." Give it a try and see how you like it. But be careful; you might just find it's addictive!

Chris Calwell
Energy Program / Atmospheric Protection Initiative
Natural Resources Defense Council (NRDC)

TIPS &

TRICKS

1. NOW YOU'RE COOKING

About 2/3 of all new stoves and ovens Americans have bought in the last few years have been microwaves. In fact, more than half of all households in the U.S. now use microwaves.

BACKGROUND. When it comes to saving energy, your stove isn't as much of a mystery as it may seem. Here are a few facts and some simple tips that will help you get started.

ENERGY FACTS

• Microwaves use around 50% less energy than conventional ovens; they're most efficient for small portions or defrosting. For larger items, stove-top cooking is more efficient, particularly with gas. For large items like turkeys, microwaving is *least efficient*.

• Pressure cookers are considerably more energy-efficient than regular ovens.

•If you've got a gas oven: Pilot lights should be burning in blue cone-shaped flames. If the flames are mostly yellow, or a "jumpy blue," you're wasting gas—the stove needs adjustment. Call the PG&E gas service department.New stoves don't have pilots; they use energy-saving electronic ignition.

• Believe it or not: Every time you open your oven door during cooking, you lose 25 to 50 degrees—or more.

SIMPLE WAYS TO SAVE ENERGY

• **Test the thermostat in your oven** to be sure it measures temperature accurately. There's a pretty good chance it doesn't.

• **Check the reflectors under your stove-top burners.** The cleaner they are, the better they'll reflect heat. If you need new ones, buy quality. The best on the market can save as much as 1/3 of the energy used when cooking on top of the stove.

• **Check the seal on your oven door** to see if there are cracks or tears in it. Even a small tear or gap is room enough for a lot of heat

to escape. And it pays to keep the seal clean (to get better heat retention.)

PRACTICAL TIPS

David Goldbeck, a kitchen expert from Woodstock, N.Y., wrote and published *The Smart Kitchen*, a delightful volume full of useful advice. Here are a few of his energy-saving tips for the stove and range.

- "If you use glass or ceramic baking dishes, you can lower the baking temperature 25°, since these materials retain heat better than others."
- "Use the right-size pan for the job. Flat bottoms are best, particularly for electric and smooth cooktops."
- "Thaw frozen foods in the refrigerator first in order to reduce cooking time."
- "Lining the oven with foil can reduce indoor air pollution by keeping the interior clean. Before doing this, however, check the manual so as not to interfere with the oven's operation."
- "Clean self-cleaning ovens right after use, to take advantage of residual heat. First clean off what you can in order to hasten the process."
- "Don't cook with the door open—this common practice is quite wasteful."
- "Do not preheat longer than necessary. Ten minutes should be sufficient. Preheating is not necessary when broiling."
- "Make sure (stove-top) electric coils are working properly. A worn-out element is a real power drain."

SOURCES

***The Smart Kitchen,* by David Goldbeck. Ceres Press.** Highly recommended. To order: Write to PO Box 87, Dept. ET, Woodstock, NY 12498. $15.95, plus $2 for shipping and handling.

2. AERATE YOUR FAUCETS

According to statistics in Home Energy *magazine, we would save over 250 million gallons of water every day if every American home installed faucet aerators.*

BACKGROUND. There's a simple device you can attach to the water faucets in your home that will save an amazing amount of water and hot water energy. It's called a "low-flow faucet aerator."

FAUCET FACTS

• The normal faucet flow is 3-5 gallons of water per minute (gpm). By attaching a low-flow faucet aerator, you can reduce the flow by 50%. Incredibly, although the flow is reduced, it will seem stronger because air is mixed into the water as it leaves the tap.

• Installing low-flow aerators on kitchen and bathroom sink faucets will save hot water. It will also cut water use by as much as 280 gallons a month for a typical family of 4. That's over 3,300 gallons a year for one family. So if only 10,000 4-member families install low-flow aerators, we'll still save over 33 million gallons a year.

• Don't confuse low-flow faucet aerators with standard screen aerators (which do not reduce faucet flow rate). Ask your store clerk if you're unsure.

SIMPLE THINGS TO DO

Installing an aerator is easy—even if you're all thumbs. The ends of most modern faucets unscrew; and that's where the aerator attaches. If you have questions, ask a plumber or local hardware store for help.

• **Portable Dishwasher Alert:** If you use a *portable* dishwasher in your kitchen, don't install a low-flow aerator on the kitchen sink faucet; the reduced flow may affect the dishwasher's performance.

3. ALL WASHED UP

The average American home washing machine
is used 416 times a year.

BACKGROUND. Since it's unlikely that anyone reading this book is contemplating going back to washboards or wringers, it should pay off economically and environmentally to learn a few tips about using washing machines efficiently.

ENERGY FACTS

- Where does the energy all go? Electric washers and dryers can account for as much as 25% of the electricity you use at home (including the hot water for the wash).
- As much as 90% of the energy consumed by washing machines goes to heating the water.
- Save energy with the right soap. You probably know that few fabrics need to be washed in hot water anymore....But with today's detergents, many lightly soiled clothes can also come clean even in cold water. Cold water saves energy.
- Washing machines use about 15% of the water in homes that have them. Each wash cycle uses 32 to 59 gallons—as much as two showers.

SIMPLE WAYS TO SAVE ENERGY

- **Experiment with cold water wash and rinse cycles.** For nearly all clothes, the results will be as good as hot water wash and warm rinse, and you'll cut your energy use by half.
- **Try cold water detergents** for lightly soiled clothes. And use a low-phosphate detergent. It will help preserve our waterways.
- **Set the water level** in the washing machine to suit the size of the load—you'll save both water and energy.
- **Try washing on a "delicate" setting** instead of "regular." The motor won't have to work as hard.

4. HOW DRY I AM

In 1988, Americans bought $4 billion worth of washers and dryers!

BACKGROUND. The only thing that concerns most of us about having a clothes-dryer—once we finally get one—is where to put it. But since dryers use a considerable amount of energy, they have a big impact on the environment. So that means we've got some more energy conservation tips for you.

ENERGY FACTS

• The energy efficiency of a clothes-dryer depends on unobstructed air circulation. So the filter and exhaust hose should be kept clear.

• People often leave their dryers on longer than necessary—the clothes are already dry, but they just don't feel like going to the basement and shutting the dryer off. Here's news: overdrying clothes wears down fabric in addition to wasting energy.

SIMPLE WAYS TO SAVE ENERGY

• **Clean the lint filter in your dryer after each use.** That lets the air circulate efficiently—the harder it is for air to swirl past your clothes, the longer the dryer has to run.

• **Dry full loads, but don't overload your dryer.** The clothes need room to tumble around so air can circulate around them.

• **If your dryer has a moisture sensor setting, use it.** It will shut off the dryer automatically when the clothes are dry.

• **Dry heavy and light fabrics separately.** That way, all the clothes in the load will be done at once.

• **Don't add wet items to a load that's already partly dry.**

• **Try drying loads consecutively** to take advantage of built-up heat. And consider using the dryer during mornings, evenings and weekends—not afternoons, when energy demand peaks.

• **Try using a clothesline.** It's natural, it's old-fashioned and the energy is free. For small loads like socks and underwear, try a small indoor drying rack.

5. DIALING FOR DOLLARS

Is your thermostat accurate? If not, chances are that the temperature sensor is being affected by cold air coming though the opening where the thermostat is mounted.

BACKGROUND. Keeping control of your thermostat is one of the simplest ways you can save a great deal of energy—and money—all year round.

ENERGY FACTS

• During the winter, you can save as much as 3% of the energy your furnace uses simply by lowering your thermostat 1°F (if it's set between 65° and 72°F).

• In the summer, the process is reversed. You save 5% of the energy used by your air conditioner for every degree you raise the thermostat setting (if it's set between 70° and 82°F).

• Do you chronically forget to turn down the heat? There are low-priced, easy-to-install thermostats that adjust the temperature automatically. The simplest have built-in clocks; the more advanced models are computerized. An advanced model will, for example, turn your furnace on 30 minutes before you wake up, turn it off when you leave for work, turn it on just before you return home, and then set it for 55°F when you go to bed. Some also have a "minimum energy use" setting which monitors temperatures when you go on vacation.

SIMPLE WAYS TO SAVE ENERGY

• **Keep the thermostat under control.** Recommended winter setting: 68° in the daytime, 55° at night. In summer, turn it to 78°F.

• **Check the temperature.** Using an accurate thermometer, make sure that the temperature near your thermostat is representative of the rest of the house. If it's located in a drafty or sunny spot, you may be getting false readings and wasting energy.

• **Plug the hole** in the wall behind the thermostat with a piece of fiberglass insulation.

6. GOT A LIGHT?

Every day, Americans buy 2.2 million light bulbs.

BACKGROUND. Flicking a light switch is a simple motion. We do it dozens of times a day without thinking.

It's time to give it some thought. According to the World Resources Institute, lighting accounts for about 20% of all the electricity used in America (5% residential, 15% commercial)—and 10% of all the emissions of CO_2, the main "greenhouse gas."

So it's important to conserve energy by lighting right.

ENERGY FACTS

• Are "long-life" incandescent bulbs better for the environment? No. They're actually more inefficient than the regular ones, and can easily cost more in extra energy than they save on replacement bulbs.

• It's a trick: "Energy-saving" incandescent bulbs usually save energy simply because they put out less light than their regular counterparts. Check out the "lumens" rating on the package for actual lighting levels.

• Believe it or not: Dust on a light bulb or dirt on a glass fixture can reduce the light it gives off by 10 percent and make it seem that you need a brighter, higher wattage light.

• Even the color paint you choose can affect your energy use. A white wall reflects 80 percent of the light that hits it; a black one reflects just 10 percent. The more light the walls reflect, the greater the chance that the light can be "recycled" by striking the wall, bouncing off, and still illuminating the room.

• Opening curtains during the day will save lighting energy. Direct sunlight is 100 times brighter than the light from a strong reading lamp.

• It used to be a good idea to leave fluorescent lights on if you were just going to be out of a room for a few minutes. But new fluorescents are long-lasting, even when switched on and off frequently.

SIMPLE WAYS TO SAVE ENERGY

- **When you leave a room, turn off the lights.** That's not as silly as it sounds. People commonly think it takes more energy to turn a light back on than it does to leave it on. But that's not true.

- **Use only as much wattage as you need.** Why waste energy with extra light? If you think you can get away with a lower wattage bulb, try it out and see if it still seems bright enough.

- **Dust the bulbs** and get the dead moths out of the fixture before you try a higher-watt bulb.

- **Use fewer bulbs in multi-bulb fixtures.** Most people don't realize that one strong bulb is more efficient than several weaker ones. For example: A single 100-watt bulb uses the same amount of energy as four 25-watt bulbs, but gives off about twice as much light. And it uses less energy than two 60-watt bulbs, but yields approximately the same light. Note: For safety's sake, put a burned-out bulb in any empty sockets.

YOU CAN SAVE ENERGY WITH LIGHT SWITCHES

- If any lights in your house are frequently left on when they shouldn't be—in the garage or basement, for instance—you can install a timer to shut them off automatically. The light-timer plugs into the wall and the lamp plugs into the timer—simple!

- Light-timers are available at most hardware stores. If you're a competent do-it-yourselfer, you can install it easily.

- You can install dimmer switches wherever you only need bright light occasionally. If it's an energy-saving dimmer switch (check it out when you buy it), you'll have the option of using less energy on lighting at other times.

SOURCES

Home Lighting, Sunset Books, Lane Publishing Company, Menlo Park, CA 94025. *Though written before many of the latest improvements in lighting efficiency, this book offers great tips on choosing and using efficient lights.*

7. THE AMAZING FLUORESCENT

If every American household replaced just one incandescent bulbs with a compact fluorescent, we'd save the energy equivalent of all the energy generated by one large power plant running all year.

BACKGROUND. Believe it or not, the incandescent light bulb that most Americans use today is basically the same as the one Thomas Edison invented over 100 years ago! Hasn't science invented anything more energy-efficient? Yes. It's called a "compact fluorescent."

ENERGY FACTS

• Compact fluorescents screw into regular incandescent bulb sockets and give off the same light...for a quarter of the energy. They also last over 7,500 hours, about ten times as long as an incandescent.

• If you replace an incandescent bulb with a compact fluorescent, you'll save the equivalent of about 600 lbs. of coal over the life of the bulb. This cuts emissions of CO_2, nitrogen oxides, and sulfur—gases responsible for the greenhouse effect and acid rain—by 65 to 70%.

• Compact fluorescent light isn't like the cool white light we're used to seeing in offices and schools. It's close to the "warmth" of incandescents. Compact fluorescents with electronic ballasts come on instantly, and don't hum or flicker like other fluorescents.

• Compact fluorescent bulbs are more expensive than incandescents—about $15-$25 per bulb. But they use so little energy that they can pay you back for the purchase cost in less than two years.

A SIMPLE WAY TO SAVE ENERGY

• Install compact fluorescents in your home. Put them where lights are left on for at least 2 hours a day. Note: Compact fluorescents are slightly larger than incandescents—so they don't fit in every fixture.

• PG&E provides discount coupons toward the purchase of compact fluorescents. Call a local office for info.

8. DISH IT OUT

Dishwashers commonly use water heated to 140°F...which is hotter than any other water used in your home.

BACKGROUND. Not every one has a dishwasher—but everyone has to wash dishes. It's a surprisingly energy-intensive activity...which means there's plenty of room to conserve what we're using.

ENERGY FACTS

- 80% of the energy your dishwasher uses is for heating water.
- According to research done at Ohio State University, a load of dishes cleaned in a dishwasher requires 37% less water than washing dishes by hand, if you leave the water running.
- However, if you fill wash and rinse basins instead of letting the water run, you'll use half as much water as a dishwasher does.

SIMPLE WAYS TO SAVE ENERGY

- **Try to wash only with full loads.** The savings will surprise you.
- **Use short cycles** for everything but the dirtiest dishes. Short cycles use less energy and work just as well.
- **If your dishwasher has an air-dry setting, choose it** instead of the heat-dry setting. You'll knock 15% (and in some cases, as much as 50%) off the energy your dishwasher uses. If there's no air-dry setting, turn the dishwasher off after its final rinse and open the door. The dishes will dry without using any extra electricity.
- **Do you rinse dishes before loading them?** Use cold water. (But of course, don't waste water by letting it run continuously.)
- **If your dishwasher has a booster heater, use it** so that you can keep your hot water tank set to a lower temperature (120°F).
- **Install your dishwasher away from your refrigerator.** The dishwasher's heat and moisture make the fridge work harder. If you have to put them next to each other, a sheet of foam insulation can minimize the damage.

9. COOL TRICKS

On an average summer day, American air conditioners provide enough cold air to produce 16 trillion ice cubes.

BACKGROUND. Air conditioners have revolutionized our lives. Summer in some parts of the U.S. was once considered "a long misery." But when air conditioners became widely available in the 1950's, people found they could enjoy life regardless of the weather.

Today, 64% of American homes have air conditioning. This may be comfortable for homeowners, but not for the planet; during the summer months, air conditioners use an ever-increasing amount of all our electricity. And about 8 million new air conditioners are sold in the U.S. every year.

ENERGY FACTS

- To cool your house efficiently, your air conditioner has to be cool itself. So try to keep it in the shade. An air conditioner exposed to direct sunlight will use up to 5% more energy than a shaded one.
- Air-conditioners located on the north sides of houses generally use less energy than those on the south or west sides, where it's sunny.
- If your air conditioner's already in the sun, you can build a simple wooden shade screen for it. (But don't block the air flow).

SIMPLE WAYS TO SAVE ENERGY

- **If you've got central air conditioning:** Cool only the rooms you use. But don't close all your vents. Closing too many of them actually *reduces* operating efficiency.
- **Turn the air conditioner off** when you leave the house for several hours or more.
- **A thermostat's not a throttle.** So don't switch your air conditioner to a colder setting when you turn it on. It won't cool the room any faster, but it *will* waste energy when you forget to turn it back up.
- **Put a timer on your room air conditioner,** or use a programmable thermostat on your central air conditioner. You don't need to leave

your air conditioner on all day to have a cool house when you get home. Hardware stores sell timers that will automatically start your air conditioner shortly before you get home. You may never notice the difference...until you see the savings on your electric bill.

•**Keep The Heat Out.** Minimize the amount of heat entering your home from outside by drawing shades and curtains on hot days. And don't leave windows and doors open while your air conditioner is running.

•**Set the thermostat as high as possible;** the minimum recommended energy-efficient summer temperature is 78°F.

CARING FOR COILS

• You can save energy by taking care of air conditioner coils. They won't work efficiently unless they're clean and straight. So check them out every spring.

• If the coils are bent, you can carefully straighten them with a plastic spatula. Or call a service person to repair them.

• If they're dusty, dirty or clogged with old leaves, you can vacuum them with your household vacuum cleaner. If the attachment on the vacuum won't fit between the coils, reverse the air flow and blow the dirt away instead.

DON'T FORGET THE FILTER

• Air conditioners are equipped with a filter to protect its fan blades, the motor and other internal parts.

• A clogged filter will use up to 5% more energy than a clean one. So check your filter at the beginning of the cooling season.

• Permanent filters can be cleaned according to the manufacturer's instructions; disposable filters should be replaced every month or two while the unit's in use.

SOURCE

Air-Conditioning & Refrigeration Institute. 1501 Wilson Blvd., 6th floor, Arlington, VA 22209. (703) 524-8800. *Has a number of free booklets that explain air conditioners, filters, and heat pumps. Be sure to send a self-addressed, stamped envelope.*

10. REFRIGERATOR MADNESS

America's refrigerators use 7% of the nation's total electricity—the equivalent of more than 50% of the power generated by all of our nuclear power plants!

BACKGROUND. What do you know about your refrigerator? Probably not much besides what's in it.

Your refrigerator does a lot more than keep your food cold. Believe it or not, it's affecting the Earth right now—using more electricity than any other appliance in your kitchen. Here are some simple tricks that can help you operate it efficiently.

ENERGY FACTS

- If you live in a city, the chances are that your refrigerator accounts for 25% of your electricity use!
- The condenser coils behind or underneath your refrigerator help it get rid of the heat it takes out of the food compartment. When dust or pet hair builds up on the coils (and it inevitably does), they don't work as efficiently, so the refrigerator motor has to work harder—which means it uses more energy.
- Not only does your refrigerator use more energy than any other home kitchen appliance, it's full of chlorofluorocarbons (CFCs), the gases that destroy the ozone layer, as well.
- Where are the CFCs? There are some in the coils, just like in an air-conditioner. But according to the Natural Resources Defense Council, there are nearly four times as many CFCs in the foam insulation that's built into the sides of the appliance.

SIMPLE WAYS TO SAVE ENERGY

- **Keep your refrigerator and freezer at the right temperature.** If they're only 10°F colder than necessary, your energy consumption will go up an amazing 25%. By keeping an eye on the temperature, you can keep a lid on energy use. The refrigerator should be between 38° and 42°F and the freezer between 0° and 5°F.

• **Make sure the door is sealed tightly.** If it's not, you're wasting energy. Check the gasket (rubber seal) for cracks and dried-on food. One way to test the seal: Close the door on a piece of paper and try to pull the paper out. If it slides out easily, it's a sure sign that cold air is escaping from inside. Adjust or replace the seal.

• **No sweat.** Use the "power-saver" switch if your refrigerator has one. It controls small heaters built into the sides of the cabinet to keep water droplets from forming on it in humid weather. Turn the heaters off except when it's humid.

• **Keep the condenser coils clean.** Brush or vacuum them at least twice a year to make them more energy-efficient. Note: Don't use a sharp instrument; you might puncture the coils.

• **Junk it right.** When it comes time to retire your refrigerator, call your local recycling center or garbage collector to see if anyone in your area can capture the CFCs in the fridge before it's junked. Putting your old refrigerator in the garage to keep sodas cold is inefficient from every standpoint except convenience. The refrigerator coils will get dirty faster and the summer heat in the garage will rot the gasket very quickly.

FOOD FACTS

Did you realize that the food you put in your refrigerator can actually affect its energy efficiency? For instance:

• It's better to keep your refrigerator and freezer as full as you can because food retains cold better than air. But don't overcrowd it; the cold air needs to circulate.

• Capping liquids keeps down the humidity inside the refrigerator, shortens the defrosting cycle, and keeps food moist longer.

• Letting warm leftovers cool before putting them away is energy-efficient.

• You can move food you need to defrost from the freezer to the refrigerator a day before you need it. That way, the frozen food gives the motor a break in cooling the refrigerator as it thaws.

11. HOW'S IT HANGING?

An uninsulated drape can cut 1/3 of the heat lost through a window. An insulated drape can reduce it by half.

BACKGROUND. Not all energy-saving methods involve sophisticated technology....Or any technology at all, for that matter.

Believe it or not, a few well-placed pieces of cloth will help cut the amount of energy you use for heating or air-conditioning your home. Drapes, window shades and blinds can be an effective way to keep your home more comfortable *and* environmentally sound.

ENERGY FACTS

• Drapes save energy effectively *only* if they fit tightly against the window and the floor. Usually this means "a valance at the top, side guides, and a weighted hem." Or: "try adding in edge seals such as Velcro or magnetic strips."

• If you install window covering on a window that faces north, you could save some 2-3% of your home heating and cooling cost. The savings increase significantly if you put the same covering on south and west facing windows.

• Other window coverings can be effective energy savers (but only if they fit tightly on the windows). Even a vinyl shade can cut heat loss in half. More elaborate shades, such as quilted curtains, can cut those losses by 80%. Venetian blinds, however, are the least effective energy savers, because they have so many gaps.

SIMPLE WAYS TO SAVE ENERGY

• **Use your drapes.** Open them on sunny winter days to let warm sun in; close them on winter nights to keep the heat in; close them on hot summer days to help keep the sun out.

• **Add an insulating lining to your draperies.** Check your local drapery shop or fabric store.

• **Install white blinds** on the south and west-facing windows to keep the sun from broiling your house in the summer. Better yet, put them outside the house to keep the wall and window shaded.

12. LIGHTS OUT

Every year, Americans buy an estimated 2.7 million light bulbs just to illuminate porches and backyards.

BACKGROUND. If you're interested in energy-efficient lights, but aren't quite ready for compact fluorescents (or any other "weird" energy-savers) in your home, there's another alternative: Put an efficient bulb *outside*, on your porch or walkway.

This is a comfortable way to get experience with energy-saving light bulbs.

ENERGY FACTS

• Most people use 60-watt incandescent bulbs on their porches or in their backyards. But incandescents are about the least efficient way to light, and they burn out after only 750-1000 hours.

• Reflectorized flood lights are also common. They're roughly as inefficient as incandescents, and consume as much as 150 watts each!

• Both types can easily be replaced by bulbs that do the same job but use1/4 of the energy.

• Buyers beware: Most of the "outdoor lighting" in hardware store ads are quartz fixtures, which typically sell for $20-30. Watch out for the energy cost—these usually take 300-500 watts each. It's a low initial price, but you pay continually high electric costs.

SIMPLE WAYS TO SAVE ENERGY

• **Use a compact fluorescent bulb** with the fixture you already have. It takes about 1/4 of the energy that an incandescent uses, and lasts ten times as long.

• **Use a metal halide bulb.** You can find one at almost any home improvement or hardware store. It gives you seven times the light for half the energy.

• **High-pressure sodium bulbs** provide up to seven times the light of an incandescent for half the cost. The initial cost is high, and a special fixture is required. But it'll last 24,000 hours.

• **Put outdoor lights on a timer or photocell control.** This way they operate only when needed.

13. SPACEHEATERS: THE FINAL FRONTIER

All 1500-watt electric spaceheaters—no matter how they look or how big they are—put out exactly the same amount of heat.

BACKGROUND. If you feel a little chill, but you don't feel like cranking up the heat...Or if the heat's already on, and it's just not keeping you warm enough, what do you do?

Millions of Americans haul out their portable space heaters. But even as they're gratefully thawing out, many of them wonder whether they're using energy wisely.

ENERGY FACTS

• A space heater is cheaper to run than your furnace. The space heater can cost up to 25¢ an hour to run; if your furnace ran for an hour, it could cost up to $1.00. Of course, you'd also be heating up the whole house, as opposed to one room.

• There are three types of space heaters.

• A quartz heater will heat an object without heating the air. "It's a direct people / wall / furniture heater," explains one expert, "rather than a room heater." It loses its effectiveness at 10-15 feet.

• A convection heater has glowing coils that are exposed to the air, or use electricity to heat a liquid. Many also have fans in them. The heater warms air in a room; if it has a fan, the fan circulates it.

• Kerosene heaters are less common. They're prohibited by law from being used in houses for safety reasons. Unvented gas appliances dump a variety of unpleasant combustion products into the air.

SIMPLE WAYS TO SAVE ENERGY

• If you've got a room you can seal off, consider using a convection heater. If you have open architecture, you probably want a "people-heating" quartz heater instead.

• Don't leave your heater on if you don't need it.

• Put on a sweater first.

14. DON'T GET SOAKED

The waterbeds in the United States consume as much power as four large power plants can produce.

BACKGROUND. Americans keep finding new ways to get ourselves into (or onto) hot water. You might be surprised, for example, to learn that there are 20 million waterbeds in the U.S.

ENERGY FACTS

- A heated waterbed can use as much energy as a large refrigerator. And according to PG&E, leaving it unmade in the fall or winter can double that by letting the heat dissipate into the air.
- Evaporation can be a major source of heat loss from hot tubs. When only 5 gallons of water evaporate, they chill the remaining 500 gallons by 1°F. Then the water has to be heated again.
- American swimming pools contain enough water to cover the city of San Francisco with a layer of water about seven feet deep. About 30 percent of that water is heated, requiring as much natural gas as a city of 600,000 normally uses.
- For every hour it's in use, an average pool heater consumes three times as much energy as a home furnace.
- Pool blankets (insulating sheets that float on the surface) cut the energy consumption of pool heaters by 40 to 70%.
- Pool pumps use about the same amount of energy in an hour as window unit air conditioners.

SIMPLE WAYS TO SAVE ENERGY

- **Cover your spa or hot tub.** Use a well-insulated cover such as "2 pound foam." It'll prevent heat loss and evaporation.
- **Use a pool blanket.**
- **Add an inch of polyethylene foam** around the edges and the bottom of your waterbed—it can cut your energy use by 30 percent.
- **At the risk of sounding like your mother... make your waterbed.** And consider using an insulated bed pad.

15. AIR-POWER YOUR SHOWER

If each member of a family of four takes a daily 5-minute shower, the family will use more than 700 gallons of water every week —a three-year supply of drinking water for one person.

BACKGROUND. For a lot of us, a long, hot shower is a guilty pleasure—it feels great, but there's a nagging suspicion we're wasting precious water.

Here's good news: There's a simple, effective way to cut shower water use by about 50%; just replace your conventional shower head with a "low flow" model. It's a good way to save natural resources *and* cash without having to do much.

SHOWER FACTS

- According to the Dept. of Energy, heating water is "the second-largest residential energy user." With a low-flow shower head, energy use (and costs) for heating hot water for showers may drop as much as 50%.
- A standard shower head uses about 5-7 gallons of water per minute (gpm)—so even a 5-minute shower can consume 35 gallons!
- "Low-flow" shower heads reduce water use by 50% or more. They typically cut the flow rate to just 3 gpm—or less.

SIMPLE THINGS TO DO

First, find out if you need a low-flow shower head:

- Use the "Milk Carton Test." Open the top of an empty half-gallon milk carton so the entire top forms a square.

- Turn your shower on fairly forcefully.

- Hold the carton up to the shower head and see how long it takes to fill with water. If it fills in less than ten seconds, your shower head's using too much water. Your shower's a candidate for a low-flow model showerhead.

Next, Take a Look at What's on the Market:
There are two types of low-flow showerheads:

• **Aerated**: Reduces the amount of water in the flow, but maintains pressure by mixing in air with the water. It feels like a standard shower, and has a steady, even spray. The only drawback: if you're tall, you may notice that the water's cooled down a little by the time it gets to your feet. This is by far the most popular type of low-flow shower head.

•**Non-aerated:** No air is mixed into the flow. It maintains heat and gets a good, forceful spray...but the flow "pulses." If you're partial to massage showerheads, this one is for you.

RESULTS

• With a low-flow shower head, four family members taking 5-minute showers each save at least 14,000 gallons of water a year. So if only 10,000 similar families were to install low-flow shower heads, we could save around 140 million gallons. And—get this—100,000 four-person families with low-flow shower heads could save 1.4 billion gallons!

• In a recent study, experts found that changing to a low-flow showerhead saved 27¢ of water a day and 51¢ of electricity for a family of four. Conclusion: Besides being good for the Earth, a low-flow shower head will pay for itself in about 2 months.

NOTE: Don't confuse "low-flows" with "water restrictors" (devices you insert into shower heads to cut flow). They're not recommended.

RESOURCES

You can find low-flow shower heads at any good hardware or plumbing supply store. In fact, PG&E gives discount coupons toward the purchase of low-flows. Call a local office for info.

Or write to

• **Resources Conservation, Inc.** P.O. Box 71, Greenwich, CT 06836. (800) 243-2862. *Has a variety of aerated low-flows.*
• **Ecological Water Products, Inc.**, 1341 West Main Rd., Middletown, RI 02840. (401) 849-4004.

HOME

IMPROVEMENTS

16. DUCT SOUP

Heating experts estimate that 99% of all houses in America with central furnaces or air conditioners have duct leaks.

BACKGROUND. If you ever think about your heating ducts at all, it's probably because they're in the way when you stack things in the basement...or because you keep banging your head on them.

But ducts are a critical part of making your home energy efficient. If they're leaking air—which they almost always do—or if they're losing heat because they're uninsulated, they're contributing as much to global warming as they are to keeping *you* warm.

ENERGY FACTS

- You can save up to 10% of your heating or cooling costs by insulating and tightening up ducts.
- Even if the air isn't actually escaping from an uninsulated duct, you lose a lot of heat through its thin metal walls.
- When the first air that comes out of the grill after you turn on the heater is chilly, and stays chilly for a long time, you know your ducts are uninsulated and you're wasting energy.

SIMPLE WAYS TO SAVE ENERGY

If your ducts aren't insulated: Turn on your furnace and feel for air escaping around the duct joints. If you feel any (and you probably will), clean around the joint, then seal with duct tape.

- Insulate the ducts with 2-inch thick fiberglass (available at home improvement stores); seal the seams with duct tape. If ducts are hard to get at, call a heating contractor.

If your ducts are already insulated: It's harder to find out if your ducts leak. You can expose the joints (where the ducts bend, for instance) to check. Or leave it to an expert.

- Before you mess with an insulated duct, check to make sure the insulation isn't asbestos (looks like heavy cloth). If it is, stay away! If you're not sure, check it with your local building department.

17. ONE MORE TIME

The U.S. recycles less than 10 percent of its trash; European countries recycle as much as 60 percent of theirs.

BACKGROUND. We all use products made from natural resources—paper, aluminum, glass. And we've all heard that recycling them saves trees, spares land, and conserves scarce space in our garbage dumps. But one of the hidden benefits of recycling is the energy that it saves.

MAKING NEWS

- Making recycled paper uses 30 to 55 percent less energy than making paper out of new trees.
- Another way to look at it: if you recycle a foot-tall stack of newspapers, you save enough energy to take a hot shower every day for a week. And considerable energy is saved by not having to truck garbage from cities to distant landfills.
- Other benefits of recycling: 95 percent less air pollution, and one tree saved for every 150 pounds of paper you recycle.
- Americans already recycle 24 million tons of paper a year—29 percent of the paper we use. That's a good start, but there's lots of room to improve. Over 50 million tons worth of room, in fact.
- For every household that recycles its daily newspaper, five trees are spared every year.

A GLASS ACT

- Recycled glass uses only two-thirds the energy needed to manufacture glass from scratch.
- That means for every soft drink bottle you recycle, you save enough energy to run a television set for an hour and a half.
- Refillable bottles don't need to be melted down before they're reused, so they save four times as much energy, according to a study for the Commission of European Communities.
- Only 27% percent of the glass used in the U.S. is recycled. But there's no reason it can't be higher.

YES YOU CAN

- It takes an incredible amount of electricity to refine aluminum from its ore. That's why most aluminum plants are located in places with cheaper electricity, like the Pacific Northwest.
- Recycling aluminum requires only a tenth as much electricity as making the same aluminum from virgin bauxite ore.
- Throwing away an aluminum can wastes as much energy as if you filled the can half full of gasoline and poured it on the ground.
- It takes barely as much energy as there is in a tablespoon of gasoline to recycle that can.

SIMPLE WAYS TO SAVE ENERGY

- Recycle! Set up a place to save newspaper, glass and aluminum.
- Separate them from your garbage. Check with your local recycler whether to sort the colored and clear glass separately.
- Recycle the paper, aluminum and glass however it's done in your area—at supermarkets, by curbside pick-up, at recycling centers.
- If you're really inspired, organize a fundraising drive to collect recyclables and put the proceeds toward your favorite charity. Or, if there isn't yet a recycling program in your community, set one up.
- When you have the choice, buy recycled products instead of ones made of virgin materials.
- Urge your local newspaper to print on recycled paper.

SOURCES

Paper Recycling Committee, American Paper Institute, 260 Madison Ave., New York, NY 10016. (212) 340-0600. *Free pamphlets on recycling paper.*

Glass Packaging Institute, 1801 K St. NW, Washington, DC 20006. (202) 887-4850. *Free pamphlets about glass recycling.*

Environmental Defense Fund, 1616 P St. NW, Washington, DC 20036. *Their book,* Coming Full Circle, *offers a good approach to setting up a recycling program. Lots of inspiring examples. Cost: $10.*

18. THE GREAT ESCAPE

The gaps you can find around the windows and doors of the average American house are the equivalent of a hole in the wall that measures 3 feet by 3 feet.

BACKGROUND. Hey...Psst...your house is leaking. There are cracks all over the place. Your doors and windows don't quite meet their frames; there are tiny spaces where the walls *almost* join the floor; there are open areas around your electrical and plumbing outlets.

And these little gaps eat energy. In fact, an amazing amount of heat in the winter—or cool air in the summer—escapes through them. But you have two simple weapons to fight with—caulking and weatherstripping.

ENERGY FACTS

- If every gas-heated home were properly caulked and weatherstripped, the natural gas saved would be enough to heat 4 million homes.
- Caulking and weatherstripping an electrically heated home can keep some 1,100 pounds of CO_2 out of the air. So if 1,000 of these homes were weatherized, over a million pounds of CO_2 would be saved.
- About 15 percent of the energy you use for heating your home goes to warming up air that leaks in through the cracks.
- People are concerned that although weatherstripping may save energy, it will keep fresh air out of their homes. While it's true that some ventilation is necessary, it's really not much of a problem—a typical house may get twice as much fresh air as it needs.

CAULKING VS. WEATHERSTRIPPING

- Cracks without any moving parts—like the places where a wall in your house meets the outside edge of a window frame, or two other dissimilar materials come together—can be sealed with caulk.
- The places where doors and windows close into their frames can

be sealed with weatherstripping—cleverly designed strips of felt, rubber, metal or plastic that fill the spaces between the frame and the doors and windows, and compress when you shut them.

• Weatherstripping materials come in many styles. Some are self-sticking, so you don't even need a hammer to install them. Others must be nailed on. Still others are crafted so pieces on the frame and the door lock together when the door closes.

• One of the trickiest places to weatherstrip is where the door meets the threshold. Special "shoes" and "sweeps" are available to stop these air leaks.

• Besides saving energy, weatherstripping and caulking have an additional benefit: By stopping drafts, they'll make your home more comfortable.

LEAK PATROL

• Some evening, when your house is at least 20° warmer than the outdoors, hold your hand up to various places around window and door frames. If you feel any drafts, they need weatherstripping.

• You can also use a candle to look for drafts. Hold the flame near the places you think might have cracks; if the flame flickers or dances, you've found a place to seal. Note: Don't burn the house down; keep flames away from all flammable objects.

SIMPLE WAYS TO SAVE ENERGY

• Weatherstrip around doors and windows.

• Seal leaks around electric switches and outlets. Gaskets are available that fit behind the switch plates and keep out a surprising amount of draftiness. Don't underestimate this one.

• To hold loose window panes in place and seal them, use window putty (also called glazing compound), available at hardware stores.

• Install "sweeps" or "shoes" to stop air from sneaking in under outside doors. If the crack under your door is too wide for store-bought weatherstripping, make a cloth "worm," fill it with sand, and lay it against the bottom of the door to keep the wind out.

• For more info: Pick up a copy of PG&E's booklet, "Do-It-Yourself Home Improvements."

19. THE UNKNOWN ATTIC

Summertime temperatures in a poorly vented attic can reach 150°...or more!

BACKGROUND. What have you got stashed in your attic? An old bowling ball? A prom dress? A pile of family photos?

You can save a substantial amount of money and do the environment a big favor by getting to know your attic a little better. Here are a few facts that might help.

ENERGY FACTS

• In the summertime, stuffy attics can add tremendously to your air-conditioning needs. Your attic heats up in the sun, and the hot attic air warms the rooms beneath, even if the attic is insulated. Rooms under poorly vented attics are 10° hotter than if the attic were well vented.

• Whole-house fans can also be installed in the attic or ceiling to pull fresh air through the house (usually at night, when it's cool outside) and make air-conditioning unnecessary.

• In most attics, pipes, ducts, dropped ceilings and electrical conduits enter the attic from the living space. When the weather is cold, these make easy escape routes for the warm air in your house.

SIMPLE WAYS TO SAVE ENERGY

• **Make sure your attic is well-insulated.** It may even make sense to add to existing insulation.

• **Seal holes** where conduits and pipes enter the attic and along partition walls, eaves, knee walls. Use caulk or compressed fiberglass insulation.

• **Check to see that your attic is well-ventilated.** Look for unclogged, screened vents near gables or roof line, and under eaves.

• **If you air-condition, consider adding roof vents.** In places with regular summer breezes, you can use a simple "turbine vent" that is spun by the wind.

20. IT'S YOUR LOSS

Heat loss through a basement floor can account for nearly a third of your heating bill.

BACKGROUND. What's going on down in your basement? Maybe you're wasting energy and harming the environment without realizing it.

ENERGY FACTS

• Heat rises, right? Actually, building scientists have found that a remarkable amount of heat sinks through the uninsulated floors of a home, into the basement.

• Cold air often enters basements through cracks in the foundation—which is especially costly if the basement is used as a heated room.

• Energy travels through many basements in hot water pipes and heating ducts. If they're uninsulated, cold basement air will rob them of heat.

SIMPLE WAYS TO SAVE ENERGY

• **Insulate under the floor.** It's the most effective way to save energy down below, provided your basement isn't heated.

• **Insulate hot water pipes and heating ducts.**

• **Install a rug with a pad.** It can work wonders in keeping the frost off your toes—and cut your energy use at the same time.

• **If you have a heated basement:** patch cracks in the foundation to keep cold air from leaking in. Then insulate basement walls.

• **If your basement is unheated:** use caulk to seal up the spaces around heating vents, the holes where telephone wires dive under the floor, and around pipes or other openings.

• **Insulate your crawl spaces.** If you can't squeeze in, call a contractor and leave the crawling to them.

Note: The vents under your house are there for a reason—to let moisture escape and prevent rot. Don't block them off.

21. SHOP SMART

Over its 15- or 20-year lifetime, the electricity to run a refrigerator costs several times as much as the refrigerator's purchase price.

BACKGROUND. A lot of the ideas included in this book can help you to use your *existing* appliances more efficiently. But some of the greatest gains in efficiency are possible when your appliances wear out and need to be replaced. "Shopping smart" is a great way to help save the environment at home.

ENERGY AND APPLIANCES

• Efficiency counts. The most efficient new appliances typically use 50% less energy than the most wasteful ones.

• For example, spark ignition instead of a pilot light can cut a stove's gas use by 40 to 50%.

• Convection ovens, which use fans to distribute heat evenly, are more efficient and 30% faster than standard models.

• Be sure to check out the EnergyGuide labels, required by law on all major appliances except clothes dryers. The labels show how the appliance's energy use stacks up against similar models.

• Buy the most efficient unit you can: high efficiency will pay off in your utility bills. And make sure it's the right size for your needs. Generally, the larger the unit, the more energy it uses.

FRIDGE FACTS

• According to Worldwatch, "Every year, the average American refrigerator consumes electricity generated from almost exactly as much coal as could be packed inside it; the most efficient model available uses about a freezer full."

• Some refrigerators have heaters to keep gaskets from sticking, to defrost, and to keep condensation from forming on the outside of the refrigerator. Newer models use their heaters more efficiently.

• Choose a refrigerator with a freezer on top, instead of a side-by-side unit. On average, the savings amount to 20%.

DISHWASHER DATA

• Look for a dishwasher with an air-dry setting. It can cut your dishwashing energy use by up to 50%.

• Choose a model with a built-in heater to boost the water temperature. Then you can lower your water heater setting by 10°F—which will cut your water heating energy use by up to 6%.

• Models with short-cycle options can save up to 25% on hot water and electricity when washing lightly soiled loads.

IN THE LAUNDRY

• Look for clothes washers with adjustable water levels and temperature controls so you use only as much as you need.

• Look for a dryer with "moisture sensors" when you're shopping. These sensors turn the dryer off automatically when your clothes are dry and can cut energy use 10 to 15%. Moisture sensors are more efficient than temperature sensor controls or standard timers.

• Cool-down cycles will tumble your clothes in cooler air during the last 5 minutes of the drying cycle, saving energy and reducing wrinkles at the same time.

AIR-CONDITIONER TIPS

• Room-sized air-conditioners are labeled with an Energy Efficiency Rating (EER) number. The higher the EER, the better. Ten is good, 11-12 or above is excellent. The label also lists a range of EERs for other units of about the same cooling capacity.

• Central air-conditioners have a similar rating known as the SEER. (The S stands for Seasonal.) An SEER of 12 is good, 14 or more is better.

• Choose the right size unit for your needs. Measure the area you want to cool, count the windows and doors and ask your dealer for suggestions.

SOURCE

"The Most Energy-Efficient Appliances," published annually by The American Council for an Energy Efficient Economy, 1001 Connecticut Ave NW, Suite 535, Washington D.C. 20036. *Cost is* $3. *A truly an invaluable resource when shopping for new appliances.*

22. INSULATE

If just 10,000 natural gas customers insulated their attics, 50 million fewer lbs. of CO2 could be released into the air each year. If the homes were heated electrically, it could be 140 million lbs.

BACKGROUND. If there's one bit of energy advice you've heard constantly, it's "Insulate your home." But insulate it where? And how? It doesn't have to be a mystery.

WHAT IS INSULATION?

- Insulation works by trapping small pockets of air as buffers between warm and cold zones inside and outside your house—the same way clothes keep you warm by trapping a layer of air between you and your shirt or sweater.
- Insulation can be made of a number of different materials—cellulose (shredded newspapers—a great way to recycle), fiberglass or rigid plastic foams of various sorts.
- Insulation is measured by its "R-value"—its resistance to heat flow. If you double the R-value, you cut heat loss in half.
- According to *The Sunset Home Energy Book*, about 60% of the energy you need to heat your home in winter escapes through the parts that can be insulated—the walls, ceiling and floor.
- Attic insulation—the most important—can save 20-35% in heating costs, and up to 15% on air-conditioning costs.

STAY DRY

- When insulation gets wet, it loses most of its insulating value—just like wet clothes.
- If water vapor gets into the insulation, chances are that some of it will condense there and soak the insulation.
- That's why it's important to install a "vapor barrier" on the inside face of insulation to keep warm, moist air from the house from infiltrating into the insulation and dampening it. It'll also keep the wood in your walls or attic from getting wet and rotting.

SIMPLE WAYS TO SAVE ENERGY

Find out if your home is insulated

• Look between the joists in the attic—the place that's most likely to be insulated. Make sure the insulation is dry and that it's spread out evenly through the attic. See how thick it is. Ask your local home improvement center to identify it; they can tell you the R value that's already there.

• To look for insulation in your walls, turn off the power to an electric outlet in an outside wall. Take off the switch plate, and shine a flashlight into the opening to see if there is anything besides air between the studs. Also, touch the wall and see if the surface is cold on a cold evening.

• Check in your basement: the insulation might be between the floor joists, or draped down the foundation walls.

How much is enough?

• In Northern California, the Department of Energy recommends 10 to 12 inches of fiberglass insulation in attics, 6 inches in floors, and 4 inches in walls—slightly more for cellulose insulation.

• The attic is one place where it may be worthwhile to add more insulation.

If you're ready to insulate

• Attics and basements are easiest to insulate, and are within comfortable reach of the do-it-yourselfer. Make sure to wear gloves and use a respirator for safety's sake.

• Insulating walls in existing homes involves drilling holes between each set of studs and blowing in insulation—a job for an experienced contractor. It's often best left until it's time to repaint the building.

• Never compress batts of insulation. Remember: it's the air spaces in the insulation that keep you warm. Compressing them means less air, so less insulating value.

• Call PG&E to find out if you qualify for their weatherization assistance program. Whether you own your home or rent it, you may be able to have it insulated at no cost.

23. THE LAWN RANGERS

An acre of lawn needs 27,000 gallons of water every week.

BACKGROUND. You might not think that landscaping and lawn care have anything to do with energy. But, as Sierra Club founder John Muir said, "Everything is hitched to everything else."

ENERGY FACTS

• During the summer, the majority of household water is used for keeping yards green.

• Water pumping is one of the largest uses of electricity in the arid Western states. So every drop of water we conserve also saves electricity. This means less CO_2 in the air.

• Even in places where water doesn't have to be moved long distances from source to tap, a significant amount of energy is required to treat and process it before it enters the water mains.

SIMPLE WAYS TO SAVE ENERGY

Treat your lawn right:

• Set your mower blades so they cut grass about 2 to 3 inches tall. Mowing it shorter dries out the soil faster and increases water use.

• Let grass clippings turn into mulch. During dry periods, cut the grass high and leave the clippings on the lawn to keep it from drying out—thus reducing the amount of water your lawn needs.

• Lawns should be watered in the morning, to reduce evaporation. Watering at night will keep evaporation down, but may encourage mold to grow.

• Most lawns need about 1 inch of water a week once they're established. Apply it slowly so the water doesn't run off.

• Here's how to tell how long it takes to apply an inch of water: Set two or three cans out on the lawn and turn on the sprinkler.

Check every few minutes to see how long it takes to land an inch in each can. Average the times for the cans, and that's the length of time to water.

WATERING SMART

• Water in the early morning or very late afternoon to cut down on how much water evaporates before it reaches the roots.

• Try drip irrigation for shrubs and garden plants. It's a way of putting the water in small, steady amounts right to the soil around the plant you're watering.

• When you re-landscape, group together the plants that need similar amounts of water. That way, you can avoid overwatering one just to irrigate another.

GOING NATIVE

• Consider plants for your yard that don't require a lot of water. These are often plants that are native to your area, because they didn't get watered when they grew wild. Investigate the new branch of landscaping science called Xeriscaping, which deals with this.

• Take the unique climate of your area into account when you plant in your yard. Any plants that are adapted to your local conditions require less water—and less attention.

• Think about shrubs, succulents and trees as a substitute for some of your lawn. Nothing requires more water than a lawn.

• When you're ready to reseed or resod your lawn, look for grasses that require less water to thrive.

SOURCES

• **Water-Conserving Plants and Landscapes for the Bay Area.** A book that shows how you can get into Xeriscaping. It's available through any East Bay Municipal Utility District business office, for $8.00 plus tax. Or write for more information: EBMUD, 3189 Danville Blvd., Alamo, CA 94507-1919.

• Check other water utilities for information specific to your area.

24. CARPOOLING

Private automobiles account for more than 20% of America's carbon dioxide emissions, 34% of our acid rain-causing nitrogen oxides, and 27% of our smog-related hyrdocarbons.

BACKGROUND. We live in a mobile society; we count on being able to go where we want, when we want. For most Americans, that means driving.

It also means using lots of energy.

The impact of the automobile is too great to ignore. Cars add significantly to the greenhouse effect, acid rain, and smog. Here are a few things we can do to lessen the effect of our driving on the environment.

ENERGY FACTS

• Our cars use more gasoline each year than the entire U.S. oil industry produces. We now import 52% of our oil, even more than we did before the oil crises of 1973 and 1979.

• Look around when you drive: most cars on the road carry only one person. In fact, we have so much *extra* room in our 140 million cars that everyone in Western Europe could fit in them with us.

• With each car carrying so few people, our roads are getting more and more crowded. Today, traffic congestion wastes about 3 billion gallons of gas a year—a lifetime supply of gasoline for an estimated 600,000 cars.

• The efficiency of your car is a significant factor in how it affects the environment. Fuel-efficient cars typically give off fewer of the emissions that contribute to global warming, smog and acid rain than less efficient ones.

• You don't have to sacrifice comfort to save gas. In 1987, the average car used 43% less gas than it did in 1978, even though it had the same amount of interior room.

SIMPLE WAYS TO SAVE ENERGY

• **Keep your car tuned up**—it's the easiest way to go the same distance on less gas. A well-tuned car uses up to 9% less gasoline than

a poorly tuned car. By making your engine burn cleaner and smoother, a tune-up can lower your tailpipe emissions and help your engine last longer.

• **Keep track of gas mileage.** If it drops quickly, you can have your car checked for a problem. It also allows you to see what you're spending each year on gasoline.

• **Zero in on zero mpg.** When your car is idling in traffic or warming up, it gets zero miles-per-gallon. Even sitting still for 60 seconds uses more gas than shutting off the engine and restarting it.

• **Think inflation.** The costs of driving around on deflated tires are staggering. Americans waste up to 2 billion gallons of gasoline a year because of under-inflated tires. Just keeping your tires inflated to their rated pressure or slightly above can improve your gas mileage by up to 5% and extend your tires' life.

• **Lighten up.** Check your trunk for unnecessary weight. Just carrying around an extra 100 pounds can raise your gasoline use 1%.

• **Consider re-tiring.** Radial tires improve gas mileage by up to 10% on the highway, 5% in the city.

• **When you shop for a new car, find out what gas mileage it gets.** The law requires it to be listed on the sales tag; if you're buying it second-hand, ask the previous owner for his or her records.

STAY OUT OF A JAM

• Try public transportation. Many car commuters read the newspaper before they leave home and read reports after they get to work. By taking reading material along on the subway or bus, you can sleep later and still be ahead of the game when you get to work.

• Look into carpooling. Some employers and local governments have set up systems to help people to find other commuters to share rides with.

• Consider walking or biking once a week on a trip when you would normally drive. Besides saving energy, it's good exercise.

• If every commuter car in the U.S. carried just one more person, we'd save 600,000 gallons of gasoline (and 12 million pounds of CO_2) every single day.

25. TANKS A LOT

In the average American home, the water heater is the second largest energy user.

BACKGROUND. As long as you can get a hot shower in the morning, you probably don't think too much about your water heater.

But this mysterious appliance has a huge impact on the environment. It consumes about 20% of the energy used in American homes.....and considerable resources have gone into manufacturing the estimated 100 million of them now in operation.

Maybe it's time to pay a little bit of attention to getting ourselves out of environmental hot water.

ENERGY FACTS

• Between 15 and 30 percent of the energy your water heater uses goes to keeping a tank of water hot, just in case you need it.

• Hot water heaters have adjustable thermostats. For every 10°F you lower the water temperature, you can save 6 percent of your water heating energy.

• The heat that escapes through the sides of the tank is especially important if it's in an unheated spot like a basement or back porch. A water heater blanket can save from 5 to 10 percent of the energy you've been using.

• Tankless water heaters are making their appearance in America these days in kitchens and bathrooms. They light up whenever someone turns on the hot water, and heat the water as it passes through—so they don't waste any energy keeping a tank hot. On the other hand, they can have pilot lights, which waste energy. So you can take your pick.

SIMPLE WAYS TO SAVE ENERGY

• **Adjust the temperature setting on the heater to 120°.** (Dishwashers without their own heaters need 140° water.) Use a thermometer, don't rely on the dial of the heater. They're generally inaccurate.

• **Put your hand on your water heater.** If it feels warm, install an insulating blanket around it, available at hardware stores. The colder the area it's in, the greater the heat loss. So if it's in the garage in the winter, you're going to lose a lot of heat. Be practical—get a heater blanket.

• **Insulate the hot water pipes leaving the tank** (for at least the first five feet—keep insulation three inches away from gas flues), wherever they are accessible. Foam sleeves or adhesive-backed foam tape are available at hardware stores.

• **Install a heat trap**—a U-shaped detour in the pipe leaving your water heater—to keep hot water from circulating through the line when no one is using water.

RESULTS

• If just 10,000 households lowered the temperature of their water heaters by 10°F, we would avoid spewing about 3 million pounds of CO_2 into the atmosphere.

SOURCES

Larry Weingarten, Elemental Enterprises, P.O. Box 928, Monterey, CA 93942. (408) 394-7077. He may be America's top authority on water heaters, and he loves to talk about them. He's asked us to include his phone number, in case you have a question.

26. HERE'S LOOKING THROUGH YOU, KID

The amount of energy that escapes through American windows every winter is the equivalent of all the oil that flows through the Alaska pipeline each year.

BACKGROUND. Your windows do more than let light into your house. During the summer, they also let heat in; and during the winter, they let it out. So it's fair to say that a lot of America's energy goes right out the window.

PANE-FUL FACTS

• Twelve times as much heat escapes from your house through a single-pane window as through a typical wall.

• Even during a mild winter, you can lose as much energy through one single-pane window as a 75-watt light bulb uses running seven hours a day, 365 days a year.

• A double-pane window retains twice as much heat as a single-pane window.

• New window coatings (thin films that are sprayed or baked on the windows during the manufacturing process) have been developed that reflect heat back into the house, but let the sunlight through easily, cutting energy losses through windows to one-sixth of what they'd be without the coating.

SIMPLE WAYS TO SAVE ENERGY

Install storm windows.

• If you feel thrifty and don't mind plastic on your windows, you can make effective storm windows by tacking clear polyethylene plastic over the outside of your windows.

• Retrofitting storm windows may not be cost-effective (depending on where you live), but they will save some energy and increase your comfort. Some types are attached in the fall and removed in

the spring; others can stay on year-round and open just like the regular windows.

Install new windows.

- Specially-made double-pane windows are now available either with an insulating air-space between the 2 panes or filled with a gas such as argon. In climates with colder winters, these can save a lot of energy.
- They're generally practical only if you're building a new house or remodeling. (It's a lot cheaper to put them in the first time than to replace old windows.)
- Frames are important. Standard aluminum frames leak twice as much heat around the edges of the glass as do the best wooden frames.

Getting reflective:

- Window films stick onto the inside of windows to block out some of the sun's rays in the summer and keep your house from overheating. They can easily be applied to existing windows. They keep out the winter sun just the same, so they make the most sense in areas where summer cooling is a bigger concern than winter heating.
- A wide variety of other products are available to bounce those incoming sunbeams back to the sky and keep them from heating up your house. There are reflective screens — essentially a mirror surface with holes cut in it so you can see out. There are louvered screens, like venetian blinds, whose slant intercepts much of the sun but little of the view. And there are fiberglass screens, which are like regular bug screens, but thicker and whiter, to send the sun back outside.

RESULTS

If just 100,000 homeowners installed one storm window, they would save some 50 million cubic feet of natural gas every year, and they'd keep more than 6 million pounds of carbon dioxide out of the air. If 1 percent of the households in the U.S. put on three storm windows, it would save one Exxon Valdez full of oil every year.

27. TUNE UP THE HEAT

If each U.S. household lowered its average heating temperatures by 6°F over a 24-hour period, we'd save the energy equivalent of 500,000 barrels of oil every day.

BACKGROUND. How important is it for you to heat your home efficiently? The American Council for an Energy Efficient Economy puts it this way: "The single most important thing people can do to save energy in their homes is to make sure their furnaces are running efficiently. More energy is used for heating than for any other purpose in American apartments and houses."

ENERGY FACTS

• According to Worldwatch, home heating is responsible for spewing 350 million tons of carbon into the atmosphere every year—which means over a billion tons of the most prevalent greenhouse gas, CO_2.

• About 12% of U.S. emissions of sulfur oxide and nitrogen oxide—both key causes of acid rain—come from home heating.

• 40% of the energy you use in your home is for heat.

• If your heating system is running inefficiently, 30-50% of the energy it uses is wasted.

SIMPLE WAYS TO SAVE ENERGY

Get a Furnace Tune-Up:

• This means testing it (for combustion efficiency and pollutants), cleaning it (e.g., dirt on the nozzle, sediment in the boiler, soot in the combustion chamber), and adjusting it (calibrating thermostats, etc.).

• Gas furnaces should be tuned every two years, oil furnaces should be tuned up annually.

• The easiest way to get a tune-up is to call a heating technician. He or she should do the whole job for around $40-$60.

• A simple tune-up can increase a furnace's heating efficiency by 5%—with a corresponding reduction in destructive emissions. Call a heating contractor for details and estimates.

• In a gas furnace, a 5% rise in efficiency means an annual savings of 8,000 cubic feet of gas. So if 100,000 families—only a tenth of a percent of U.S. households—get tune-ups, we'll save over half a billion cubic feet of gas a year.

A FEW HEATING TIPS

If You Have a Forced-Air System:

• Insulate ducts wherever they pass through unheated spaces.

• During heating season, change your air filters once a month. Your heater uses more energy when the filter is full of dust.

If You Have an Electric Heating System:

Consider installing a heat pump, which "uses thermal energy from outside air for both heating and cooling." Initial cost may seem high (as much as $2,000 for a whole-house unit, about $400 for a single room), but it can cut your heating bill by 40% a year.

If You Have a Hot Water / Steam System:

Put a reflector behind your radiator (you can buy one or make it by taping aluminum foil on cardboard). This saves energy and cash by throwing back heat you'd normally lose through the wall.

SOURCES

• Check out the booklet called "Heating Systems," available from: **Public Information Office, Massachusetts Audubon Society, Lincoln, MA 01173.** Write for ordering info.

• Buying a new heater? **The American Council for an Energy-Efficient Economy, 1001 Connecticut Ave. NW, Suite 535, Washington, D.C. 20036,** has a booklet entitled "The Most Energy-Efficient Appliances" which lists selected brand name models.

28. PLAY IT AGAIN, FAN

In the last 10 years, Americans have bought 60 million ceiling fans.

BACKGROUND. "About a hundred years ago," says *Electrical Review* magazine, " ceiling fans were introduced to make rooms more comfortable in warm climates." Today, when we think of ceiling fans, we usually think of classic films like *Casablanca*. There *is* a romance to them. But there's still a practical reason for buying one, too.

ENERGY FACTS

• Ceiling fans consume as little energy as a 60 watt bulb—which is about 98% less energy than most central air conditioners use.

• Ceiling fans are often used instead of air conditioning. But it's not necessarily one *or* the other. Fans produce air currents that carry heat away from the skin, so even air conditioned rooms feel cooler when one is running.

• Many ceiling fans save energy in winter as well as summer. The secret: their motors run in "reverse." This pushes warm air caught near the ceiling down to where you can feel it.

• How much difference can that make? Some rooms in your house can be 15 degrees warmer at the ceiling than at the floor. A well-placed ceiling fan can reduce this difference to only 3 degrees.

SIMPLE WAYS TO SAVE ENERGY

• **If you're shopping for a ceiling fan:** You'll find them at a home improvement center. Look for a fan that's reversible and has more than one speed. Check to make sure the blades are angled at least ten degrees.

• **If you're thinking about where to install one:** Rooms with the highest ceilings are the best candidates. But make sure the blades are between seven and nine feet above the floor.

• **Match the size of your fan to the size of the room.** For rooms 12 feet by 12 feet or less, you can use a 36-inch or 42-inch fan. For rooms up to 12 feet by 18 feet, use a 48-inch or 52-inch fan. If the room's bigger than that, you'll probably need at least two fans.

29. STAY ACTIVE

BACKGROUND. In this book, we've talked about how you can help save the earth by using energy wisely.

There's another kind of energy you can use to protect the environment—your own.

First, if you haven't already taken steps to make your life and home more energy-efficient, now's a good time to begin. Start small—tackle one or two tasks at a time. Call your local PG&E office to see how they can help.

Then look outside your home. Here are the name and addresses of a few of the groups that have taken an active role in energy conservation issues. They all depend on people like you to pitch in. Contact them to see how you can get involved.

Remember—whether you're using your energy to save energy in your home, or in your community—your efforts *do* make a difference.

Some groups to contact:

Environmental Defense Fund, 1616 P St. NW, Suite 150, Washington, D.C. 20036

Natural Resources Defense Council, 1350 New York Ave. NW, Washington, D.C. 20005

Renew America, 1001 Connecticut Ave. NW, Suite 1719, Washington, D.C. 20036

Rocky Mountain Institute, 1739, Snowmass Creek Road, Snowmass, Colorado 81654

Sierra Club, 730 Polk St., San Francisco, CA 94009

Note: To contact local chapters of these or any environmental organization, check your phone book or yellow pages. And don't hesitate to write to local government officials to make your wishes known.

30. SPREAD THE WORD

This book was created for one purpose—to give you a sense of the power you have to make our world a better place.

You can do it without huge sacrifices.
Choices that seem small on a day-to-day
level can have an enormous impact
...if we all act together.
We need everyone to help.

So when you're done with this book,
and you've started saving energy,
pass it on.

Remember that saving the Earth begins
with you. And one of the most
powerful things you can do is
to "spread the word."

WHAT'S

HAPPENING

THE GREENHOUSE EFFECT

Here's one way to understand the greenhouse effect: Think of a car parked in the summer sun. It gets incredibly hot inside because windows let the sunlight in, but don't let heat escape. Our atmosphere is like that. It naturally keeps the Earth warm by trapping some of the sun's heat with a blanket of gases.

The "recipe" for this blanket calls for fairly exact portions of water vapor, carbon dioxide (CO_2), methane, and a few others. They each trap a fraction of the heat escaping from the earth. Too much of any one of them causes the atmosphere to get too hot.

HOW IT USED TO WORK

Natural sources of extra "greenhouse gases," like volcanoes and animals, have always been balanced by natural absorbers of those gases, like oceans and trees. That's why our ancestors didn't cause global warming by burning wood—they were just releasing CO_2 that the trees had absorbed during their lifetimes, more or less. New trees took it up again, and everything was fine.

THE RICKETY BALANCE

Now, humans have begun to upset that balance. Not only are we cutting down more trees than we're planting, but we're burning more and more fossil fuels—reserves of oil, coal and natural gas trapped beneath the earth. These fuels were formed from the remains of ancient jungles and swamps; it took them eons to absorb the CO_2 that we release in a few seconds by burning them. Thanks to fossil fuels, the atmosphere now contains 25% more CO_2 than it did a century ago.

SO WHAT?

Scientists don't know exactly how much hotter this extra CO_2 will make the Earth. But many agree it will warm the Earth overall—by 4 to 9° F by the year 2050. That may not sound like much, but it only took a rise of a few degrees to end the last Ice Age.

This kind of warming could have disastrous effects. It could melt parts of the polar ice-caps, raising sea level by a few feet—and flooding many of the world's major cities and harbors. It could lead to more scorching

summers, droughts, and deserts. And it certainly would change weather patterns in ways we can't foresee. It could be very hard for people to adapt to a several-hundred-mile shift in the Corn Belt, to say nothing of how hard it could be for animals and plants.

THE FIVE "GREENHOUSE GASES"

• **Carbon dioxide** causes about 50% of the "greenhouse effect." The world's energy use produces about 20 *billion* tons of CO_2 each year. Another 4 billion tons comes from deforestation.

• **Chlorofluorocarbons** (CFCs), which are used as coolant in air conditioners and refrigerators, account for about 15-20% of the greenhouse effect. CFCs are completely artificial; they persist in the atmosphere for decades and contribute to ozone depletion too.

• **Methane,** the "natural gas" we use to heat our water and our homes, accounts for 18% of the greenhouse effect.

• **Nitrous Oxide**, a pollutant from cars and power plants, produces 10 percent of the greenhouse effect.

• **Ozone,** a component of urban smog, also contributes a tiny fraction to global warming.

HOW ENERGY AFFECTS THE GREENHOUSE

• A typical household uses about 7,000-10,000 kilowatt-hours (kwh) of electricity every year. Each kwh we save keeps about 1.5 pounds of CO_2 out of the atmosphere.

• Households use about 750 therms of natural gas a year, on the average. Some of it leaks out of pipes and contributes directly to the greenhouse effect. The rest produces CO_2 when it burns—about 12 pounds for every therm.

• The average car uses 500 gallons of gasoline in a year. Every gallon burned adds 20 pounds of carbon dioxide to the air.

• Even wasting water contributes to the greenhouse effect because of the energy it took to pump, purify, and treat that water. According to the Natural Resources Defense Council, about 6 pounds of CO_2 are emitted for every 1,000 gallons of water we use.

ACID RAIN

Some of the rain that falls in the northeastern U.S. is nearly as acidic as lemon juice. In parts of California, the rain and fog are not quite as tart, but still pose a serious threat. Here's what causes it:

SULFUR OXIDES

Sulfur makes up a small fraction of the coal and heavy oil used in some power plants. When these fuels are burned, the sulfur combines with oxygen in the air, forms sulfur oxides (SOx), and escapes up the smokestack.

Electric utilities emit an estimated two-thirds of the nation's SOx. The contributions from each power company depend on the fuels they burn and the pollution controls they use; PG&E burns no coal, and very little oil, to generate electricity.

NITROGEN OXIDES

Nitrogen oxides (NOx) also lead to acid rain. During the hot combustion that occurs in car engines and power plants, the nitrogen in the air can actually "burn" and form NOx. Sophisticated control technologies at power plants and in cars' catalytic convertors have reduced NOx emissions sharply since the 1970s, but the number of power plants and cars keeps growing.

HOW ACID RAIN OCCURS

The SOx and NOx mix with water in clouds to form sulfuric and nitric acids, then fall back to earth in rain or snow, making lakes and streams too acidic for fish and other animals to survive. Besides that, it attacks forests and damages agricultural crops.

HOW ENERGY USE AFFECTS ACID RAIN

- One of the best ways to reduce emissions of SOx and NOx is simply to consume less electricity. Most of the power plants that emit these pollutants are operated in direct proportion to the demand for electricity. The less you need, the less they burn.
- Likewise, the fewer gallons of gasoline you burn, the less NOx come out of your tailpipe. Your car emits most of its NOx in the minute after you first start it, before the catalytic convertor has gotten warm enough to begin controlling it. So, in addition to saving energy, avoiding short trips in your car will also help control acid rain.

URBAN AIR POLLUTION

If you live in a big city, you may be accustomed to smog, but medium and small-sized cities are starting to have bad breath, too. The Environmental Protection Agency reports that more than 100 million Americans live in places where the air is unhealthy at least a few days a year.

GASP, CHOKE, WHEEZE

As a result, more than 30,000 people in the U.S. die prematurely from lung diseases every year, according to the American Lung Association. The health costs from smog-related respiratory diseases in hundreds of thousands of people add as much as $90 billion to America's medical bill every year.

INGREDIENTS:

It takes several pollutants to form smog, including nitrogen oxides (NOx) and hydrocarbons (unburned or partially burned fuel). Both stem from the use of gasoline, natural gas, and even things like paint thinner.

Sunlight helps "cook" these chemicals into the blend we call smog. The simplest measure of smog is ozone (O_3), which is useful high in the atmosphere but harmful to humans, other animals, plants and property down near the ground.

HOW ENERGY USE AFFECTS THE AIR QUALITY

- According to the Public Interest Research Groups, our cars, trucks and buses emitted 8.5 million tons of NOx and 6.5 million tons of hydrocarbons in 1986. Not surprisingly, everything we can do to reduce our consumption of gasoline or *reduce the distance goods are transported* helps to minimize NOx emissions.

- Utilities, oil and chemical plants account for about half the national emissions of NOx and hydrocarbons. But it's misleading to blame only these big entities for the problem; they produce energy, gasoline, plastics and other energy-intensive products because of *our* demand for them. By reducing our demand, we can reduce the severity of the problem.

OZONE DEPLETION

The ozone layer is a thin, invisible shield of gases 6 to 30 miles above the ground. It protects us from the sun's ultraviolet light. But now, manmade chemicals containing chlorine and bromine have begun to attack the ozone layer. These are the chemicals:

Chlorofluorocarbons (CFCs)—used as refrigerants and aerosol propellants, in foam plastics and some solvents. Includes Freon.

Halons—used in some dry fire extinguishers.

Industrial solvents such as methyl chloroform and carbon tetrachloride—used to clean electronic circuits, and greasy engine parts.

CFC substitutes (HCFCs)—increasingly used to replace CFCs in some products. They're not as strong, but still harm the ozone layer.

OFF IN THE OZONE

Since 1969, these chemicals have reduced the strength of the ozone layer above populated areas by 3 to 6%. This has already increased the incidence of skin cancer and cataracts among people living in high northern and southern latitudes. If ozone depletion continues at the present rate, the EPA estimates, up to 300 million extra cases of skin cancer could result in the U.S. alone over the next 180 years.

HOW ENERGY USE AFFECTS THE OZONE LAYER

- Most of what we can do to protect the ozone layer involves reducing our use of the chemicals listed on the left. But some energy-saving tips can also help the ozone layer. For example, a large percentage of CFCs are used in refrigerators and home and automobile air conditioners. By saving energy through wise use of these devices, we can minimize the need to refill them with new CFCs.

- When your air-conditioner or refrigerator is drained of CFCs for servicing, it's important to capture them instead of letting them escape into the air.

- Many types of insulation (especially foam) contain CFCs. So if you insulate your home, it's critical to ask for *cellulose*, *fiberglass* or other CFC-free insulation. If we don't, saving energy can actually harm the ozone layer.

PG&E PUBLICATIONS

These publications are available free from PG&E. Ask for them at your local PG&E office.

- **Apartment Living for Less**
- **Heat and Your Heart**
- **Light It Right**
- **Windows**
- **Going on Vacation? (Also available in Spanish)**
- **Give Your Furnace Pilot the Summer Off. And Relight It in the Fall**
- **Solar Hot Water Systems for the Homeowner.**
- **Insulate. Save Energy. (Also available in Spanish)**
- **LIVE, the Senior Citizen's Guide to Energy Survival.**
- **Home Energy Survey Guidebook**
- **Trees—Planting for the Future**
- **PG&E Do-It-Yourself Home Improvements (Also available in Spanish)**
- **Choosing and Using Appliances**
- **Money Saver's Guidebook**
- **How to Check Radio and TV Disturbances in Your Home**
- **Gas and Electric Safety in Your Home**

- A Do-It-Yourself Survey for Single Family Homes (Also available in Spanish)
- A Do-It-Yourself Survey for Mobile Homes
- Home Energy Saver's Packet (Also available in Spanish)
- Naturally Cool
- Residential Energy Use Information and Services Handbook (Also available in Chinese)
- Saving Energy on the Farm
- Energy Saving Tips. A Money Guide for Small Businesses
- Your Guide to PG&E Recreation Areas
- Lakes of California
- Electric Safety from A to ZAP!
- The Professor Wattensocket Safety Book
- Electric Safety Booklet
- Natural Gas Safety Booklet
- About Safety Coloring Book
- Kite Safety Fun Book
- Keep Away from Power Lines (Also available in Spanish)
- Electrical Safety on the Farm (Also available in Spanish)
- Build Safely
- Electricity—Facts to Live By in Emergencies
- Safety or Danger—Take Your Pick